NATURAL DISASTERS

Essential Issues

Natural
Disasters

BY MARCIA AMIDON LUSTED

Content Consultant
Susan Cobb, meteorologist and science writer
NOAA National Severe Storms Laboratory

ABDO
Publishing Company

CREDITS

Published by ABDO Publishing Company, 8000 West 78th Street, Edina, Minnesota 55439. Copyright © 2011 by Abdo Consulting Group, Inc. International copyrights reserved in all countries. No part of this book may be reproduced in any form without written permission from the publisher. The Essential Library™ is a trademark and logo of ABDO Publishing Company.

Printed in the United States of America,
North Mankato, Minnesota
112010
012011

 THIS BOOK CONTAINS AT LEAST 10% RECYCLED MATERIALS.

Editor: Rebecca Rowell
Copy Editor: Lillian Dondero
Interior Design and Production: Becky Daum
Cover Design: Marie Tupy

Library of Congress Cataloging-in-Publication Data
Lusted, Marcia Amidon, 1962- , author.
 Natural disasters / By Marcia Amidon Lusted.
    p. cm. -- (Essential issues)
 Includes bibliographical references.
 ISBN 978-1-61714-775-3
 1. Natural disasters. I. Title.
 GB5014.L87 2011
 363.34--dc22

                                2010045055

TABLE OF CONTENTS

Many parts of New Orleans remained flooded four days after Hurricane Katrina made landfall in 2005.

MONSTER STORM

On August 23, 2005, a storm began forming in the Atlantic Ocean over the Bahamas. It grew in size and power, carrying large amounts of rain. The storm quickly developed into a hurricane that moved into the Gulf of Mexico and toward the Gulf Coast of the United States. By the time it approached Louisiana, the hurricane—now named Katrina—was one of the most powerful storms ever recorded. When it made landfall just southeast of New Orleans on August 29, Katrina was a Category 3 hurricane with winds of 125 miles per hour (201 km/h).

New Orleans is located near the mouth of the Mississippi River, and 80 percent of the city sits below sea level. This makes it especially vulnerable to the winds and water of a hurricane. Levees that had been built to protect areas of the city from Lake Pontchartrain failed. Storm surge from Katrina drove water into the streets that flooded many areas, especially the part of the city known as the Lower Ninth Ward.

Despite the order to evacuate New Orleans the previous day, more than 26,000 people remained in the city, trapped. Most had been unable to

Katrina's Strength

Hurricane Katrina was one of the strongest hurricanes ever recorded, with winds of 131 to 155 miles per hour (211 to 249 km/h) capable of uprooting trees and damaging structures. Katrina's highest measured wind speed was 175 miles per hour (282 km/h).

leave because they did not have the financial means to do so or were not able to find places on the public evacuation buses. Many citizens were stranded on rooftops as water flooded their neighborhoods. They waved handmade cardboard signs asking for help at the news media flying overhead in helicopters.

New Orleans

The geography of New Orleans makes the city especially vulnerable to hurricane damage. The city's elevation ranges from 5 feet (1.5 m) below sea level to 15 feet (4.6 m) above, which means it takes very little rise in the ocean level to flood the city. New Orleans is nick-named the Crescent City because of its location. It sits in a curve of the Missis-sippi River, surrounded by the waters of the river, the Gulf Coast, and Lake Pon-tchartrain, which connects to Lake Borgne and then to the Atlantic Ocean. The city has a semitropical, or subtropical, climate and receives more than five feet of rain a year.

Others floated in anything they could find, paddling to safety or to help others. Hospitals were left without power or sufficient medical personnel. Food became scarce. Hundreds of thousands of survivors were crammed into the Louisiana Superdome stadium with insufficient supplies and overwhelmed hygiene facilities. Another 20,000 had an equally dismal experience at the Ernest N. Morial Convention Center. Tony Cash spent three nights at the convention center. He described his experience: "It was as if all of us were already pronounced dead. As if somebody already had the body bags. Wasn't nobody coming to get us."[1]

In the aftermath of Hurricane Katrina, police officers and volunteers used boats to rescue residents from flooded neighborhoods in New Orleans.

Almost 2,000 people would die as a result of Hurricane Katrina. Other costs included property damage and between $60 billion and $120 billion in insurance losses. More than the human and financial losses, Katrina also created a great deal of controversy about the emergency response of the federal government.

THE COSTS OF NATURAL DISASTERS

The United States has faced other devastating natural disasters. Still, Katrina illustrated some of the major issues associated with any natural disaster: preparedness—or lack of it—response, and recovery. How these issues are handled dramatically affects the overall impact of a natural disaster.

Natural disasters include hurricanes, tornadoes, tsunamis, floods, blizzards, landslides, wildfires, earthquakes, and volcanic eruptions. These events can destroy lives and property or create circumstances that result in damage and loss of life. Natural disasters can be particularly devastating in places where governments and citizens do not have the money for preparedness because these events can be extremely costly. Beyond paying for cleanup, governments must rebuild essential infrastructures such as roads, bridges, and public buildings.

On a smaller level, homeowners and their insurance companies are faced with the costs of replacing homes and possessions. Businesses must make up for similar losses,

A History of Hurricanes

New Orleans is no stranger to hurricanes. One of the earliest recorded hurricanes in US history hit the city in 1779. It experiences either a direct hit or a brush from a hurricane every 3.7 years on average. Damaging hurricanes bash the city approximately every 12 years.

while suffering the additional loss of income during the time they work to reopen their doors to customers. Areas that rely heavily on tourism will lose that income until cleanup and rebuilding are completed. Individuals lose their jobs when businesses are forced to close for good.

Natural disasters seem to be increasing worldwide, and their costs are rising as well. According to the United Nations, in 2008, deaths and economic losses from natural

CNN Hurricane Broadcast

Three days after the storm, CNN broadcast from New Orleans. Reporters found people in desperate need of food, water, and medical attention and feeling abandoned by their government:

ANNOUNCER: This is America? Chaos, anger, a desperate city feeling abandoned.

UNIDENTIFIED CHILDREN: We want help! We want help!

ANNOUNCER: Violence, gunfire, looting, and starvation.

UNIDENTIFIED FEMALE: We can't take this. We've been out here for three days. And we've been asking for help.

ANNOUNCER: Mothers, children, the elderly, hurricane survivors still waiting for help. . . . Unbelievably, shots fired at rescuers. . . . They hope to find survivors. . . . The city's mayor is at his wits end. Today he issued a desperate SOS, saying, "Currently, the convention center is unsanitary and unsafe and we are running out of supplies for 15,000 to 20,000 people. We are now allowing the people to march." They are marching in search of food, water and relief. . . . Infants have no formula, the children no food, nothing for adults, no medical help. They're burning with frustration, and sure they have been forgotten.[2]

disasters worldwide were twice the average losses from 2000 to 2007. In 2008, 235,816 people were killed by natural disasters, 211 million people were affected by these disasters in some way, and the total cost was $181 billion.

Preparedness is the best way to combat devastation from a natural disaster. Leaders in high-risk areas must have better plans and resources in place to respond to disasters, while scientists work at better understanding how and when disasters occur and how to detect them as early as possible. Community leaders also must address how to cope successfully with these events and their consequences. Since natural disasters often occur with little or no warning, studying and learning from past disasters is one of the best ways to prepare for them in the future.

"Disaster can attack from above or below, from the clouds or the ground. Weather disasters, such as storms, floods, and drought, remind us of the precarious balance between the elements that support life on Earth. An increase or decrease in any of the atmosphere's characteristics—too hot, too cold, too wet, or too dry—can be catastrophic. Earthquakes and volcanoes, on the other hand, hint at the churning cauldron beneath our feet."[3]

— *Christine Gibson,*
Extreme Natural Disasters

Preparedness, such as planning evacuation routes, can help reduce the toll and costs of natural disasters.

Mount Vesuvius and the ruins of Pompeii

EARLY DISASTERS

Natural disasters have occurred for billions of years. They are as old as the earth. Scientists have speculated that, even before recorded history, natural disasters such as volcanic eruptions and floods shaped the earth. In addition to destroying entire communities, disasters have affected ecosystems and climates across the globe.

VESUVIUS

Some of ancient history's most notable natural disasters were caused by volcanoes. In the year 79, Mount Vesuvius erupted in the Campania region of western Italy, sending ash, pumice, and poisonous fumes over the Roman city of Pompeii.

The story of Pompeii is striking for two reasons. First, someone recorded the event. A Roman administrator and poet named Pliny the Younger wrote about what happened. His descriptions of tremors reveal the tell-tale signs of the impending eruption he witnessed. Pliny described "a fearful black cloud . . . and quivering bursts of flame . . . parted to reveal great tongues of fire, like flashes of lightning magnified in size."[1] He also noted that the sea was sucked away and forced back—this would have been a tsunami. Pliny's writings show that the citizens were not aware of these signs. Tremors in the area "were not particularly alarming because they are frequent," he wrote.[2]

Pompeii is also striking because of the eruption's aftermath. Many Pompeians died, their bodies entombed in ash and pumice. The thriving city was all but forgotten until a peasant digging a well in 1711 uncovered one of its marble walls. Archeologists began excavating the city in the 1740s. They found the city and many of its inhabitants well preserved by 19 to 23 feet (6 to 7 m) of pumice and ash.

The excavation site has provided a detailed look into life at the time of Pompeii's destruction. Researchers have learned about economic, political, religious, and social aspects of life. The site has also provided vast information about city planning. It is an invaluable resource for historians.

TAMBORA AND KRAKATAU

More than 1,700 years later, in April 1815, a monumental volcanic disaster took place in Indonesia, on the island of Sumbawa. Mount Tambora's eruption is still on record as the largest ever. Initially, 10,000 people died from the eruption and ensuing tsunamis. The disaster resulted in disease and starvation that led to the deaths of approximately

World Heritage Site

Herculaneum, Stabiae, and Torre Annunziata were also lost to Vesuvius's destruction. In 1997, the United Nations Educational, Scientific, and Cultural Organization collectively declared the ruins of Pompeii, Herculaneum, and Torre Annunziata a World Heritage site. The designation was granted "considering that the impressive remains . . . provide a complete and vivid picture of society and daily life at a specific moment in the past that is without parallel anywhere in the world."[3]

82,000 more islanders. But the disaster affected people well beyond Indonesia.

Tambora's eruption had far-reaching effects on the planet's climate and weather. The clouds of ash spewed by the volcano entered the jet stream, a current of high-speed winds in Earth's atmosphere that usually blows from the west, sometimes in excess of 250 miles per hour (402 km/h). The jet stream spread Tambora's ash around the globe, creating a veil of dust that blocked light and heat from reaching the Northern Hemisphere, including as far away as North America. This caused dramatic climate effects that devastated many living in these areas.

In New England and eastern Canada, snow fell in May and June, destroying crops. People suffered from malnutrition and starvation. In Europe, Switzerland declared a national emergency. In addition to the tens of thousands of immediate deaths caused by the eruption of Mount Tambora, as many as 48,000 people died worldwide of resulting starvation and disease.

The year 1816 became known as "the year without a summer" or "eighteen hundred and froze-to-

Moving West

The year 1816 is one reason Americans moved westward. People headed west to escape the cold, food shortages, and poverty caused by Tambora's historic eruption.

death" because of the weather changes.[4] Losses caused by the changes prompted some to call it "the poverty year."[5]

Another catastrophic eruption took place later that century when the Indonesian island of Krakatau was completely blown apart in August 1883. The explosion was heard almost 3,000 miles (4,828 km) away. A cloud of ash and dust circled Earth several times in coming years, cooling the atmosphere. More than 36,000 people died in the eruption and as a result of the tsunamis that swept across neighboring islands.

The events show how devastating a volcanic eruption can be on the environment and its inhabitants—both in the short-term and the long-term. In addition, the eruptions took place in volcanoes previously thought to be dormant, and all three are capable of erupting again.

Galveston, 1900

Hurricanes have caused considerable damage in the United States. One of the worst struck Galveston, Texas, on September 8, 1900. Galveston is an island community on the Gulf of Mexico. Some inhabitants of Galveston in 1900 felt the city needed a seawall to protect it from the ocean, but the wall was never built. As the hurricane approached, people ignored the warnings and went to the boardwalk on the beach to view the oncoming storm.

The hurricane engulfed the bridges that connected the island to mainland Texas, leaving its inhabitants cut off. With its flat terrain, the entire city was quickly submerged because there was no higher ground for inhabitants to escape to. Some survived only by climbing into boats. When the water receded, the city had lost 8,000 residents and thousands of homes.

The community learned from the deadly experience. Galveston built

Isaac's Storm

One of the few people heeding the weather warnings in Galveston on September 8, 1900, was Isaac Cline, a meteorologist with the US Weather Bureau. Cline watched the signs of the approaching hurricane, including rising sea levels, falling barometer readings, and increasing wind speed. He sent telegraphs to the Weather Bureau headquarters in Washington DC, but he did not put a notice in the local paper. Cline is said to have driven along Galveston's beaches, urging sightseers to move to higher ground.

The instruments Cline used to measure the storm were not as reliable as today's. Wind speed is thought to have reached 120 miles per hour (193 km/h) at its height, though later estimates place the speeds at 131 to 155 miles per hour (210 to 249 km/h). Cline continued to telegraph storm information to Washington DC until the telegraph lines were destroyed. His last message read, "Gulf rising rapidly; half the city now underwater."[6] As a result of the 1900 hurricane—which claimed the life of his wife—Cline would spend the rest of his life studying hurricanes.

Much of Galveston was reduced to rubble by the 1900 hurricane.

a seawall and raised the level of the city behind it. Subsequent hurricanes, including Hurricane Ike in 2008, pounded the city but did not destroy it.

San Francisco, 1906

A few years after Galveston's disaster, in the early hours of April 18, 1906, an earthquake struck San Francisco, California. The earthquake, which historians believe was probably 7.8 on the Richter scale, occurred at 5:12 a.m. and was the result of a sideways slip in the San Andreas Fault. The earth was so disrupted in some places that it made straight fences zigzag. San Francisco was at the heart of this fault slip. When shock waves went through the reclaimed swampland of one neighborhood, the man-made ground became temporarily liquefied. The ground shook so hard that in some places, buildings simply sank. Other buildings collapsed, killing those inside or on the streets below. In San Francisco Bay, the water level fell four inches (10 cm) for about 15 minutes, in a sort of negative tsunami.

The quake caused considerable damage. Gas lines broke, causing a fire that consumed more than 500 blocks—more than four square miles (10 sq km)—of the city. Many people living in flimsy wooden tenements were trapped and incinerated. Some people fled to the city's parks. Writer Jack London was working as a reporter for the magazine *Collier's Weekly* and described the scene:

> *The earthquake shook down in San Francisco hundreds of thousands of dollars' worth of walls and chimneys. But the conflagration that followed burned up hundreds of millions of dollars' worth of property. There is no estimating within hundreds of millions the actual damage wrought. Not in history has a modern imperial city been so completely destroyed. San Francisco is gone.*[7]

One-quarter of a million people were left homeless. The US Army estimated the number of deaths from the earthquake and fire at 700, but recent estimates place the number as high as 3,000. As devastating as the San Francisco earthquake was, it did have one benefit. Geologists were able to record their observations in the aftermath, and the governor of California created a commission to compile their work. The result was the first comprehensive portrait of a US earthquake, which would lead to fault-line research and the birth of earthquake science in the United States.

These examples highlight the destruction both geologic and weather or meteorologic forces can cause. Scientists and researchers have learned much about the science and history of natural disasters from these events. More recent disasters have highlighted the importance of prediction, response, and recovery.

Predicting another San Francisco Earthquake

Scientists believe another major earthquake may occur in the San Francisco area, based on the pattern of earthquakes that have taken place there since 1836. From 1836 to 1911, four to five large earthquakes shook the region, but there were no major quakes for the next 68 years. From 1979 to 1989, there were four larger earthquakes, measuring a magnitude of 6.0 or higher on the Richter scale. This has led experts to believe the probability of a major earthquake—measuring 6.8 or higher—occurring within the next 30 years is about 67 percent.

A man looks at the remains of San Francisco's city hall following the 1906 earthquake.

Rescue and cleanup workers surveyed a flooded lobby at a hotel in Thailand in December 2004 after the Indian Ocean tsunami.

Modern-Day Disasters

While events such as the eruption of Mount Vesuvius show how long natural disasters have been taking place, such occurrences are not a thing of the past. They are very much a part of recent history and current events.

During the first decade of the twenty-first century, several natural disasters occurred around the globe.

Indian Ocean Tsunami

On December 26, 2004, vacationers walking along the beach on the island of Sumatra in Indonesia were amazed to see the ocean water draining away from the shore, exposing vast expanses of sand covered with flopping fish. Tourists grabbed their cameras and native fishermen snatched up the fish for dinner. Seconds later, a wall of water 50 feet (15 km) high crashed over the beach, sweeping away people, trees, cars, and buildings. "I heard this strange thunderous sound from somewhere," a fisherman who had been swept away remembered. "A sound I'd never heard before. I thought it was the sound of bombs. It felt like doomsday."[1]

The tsunami was triggered by a 9.0-magnitude undersea earthquake that had begun off the coast of Sumatra earlier that morning. The quake caused a rupture estimated to be 600 miles (1,000 km) long and moved trillions of tons of rock. It was the largest earthquake in 40 years.

For several hours following the quake, the tsunami traveled the Indian Ocean, battering the shorelines of 11 countries. The tsunami traveled 3,000 miles (4,828 km)—reaching as far away as Africa. The Indian Ocean tsunami of 2004 was one of the most destructive in history. At least 225,000 people died and damages totaled more than $10 billion. It would launch a massive relief effort and renew efforts to establish some sort of early warning system for the area.

China, 2008

Four years later, an earthquake in China brought to light other issues related to natural disasters. On May 12, 2008, a 7.9-magnitude earthquake struck Sichuan province in western China. Approximately 70,000 people were killed, and another 18,000 were still missing a year later. Many of those killed were schoolchildren who were crushed when their schools collapsed around them. Following the disaster, there was an outcry regarding construction and the schools being poorly built.

Rigorous new rules about constructing earthquake-resistant buildings had been put into place following a devastating earthquake in 1976. Still, many public buildings collapsed, leaving people to wonder how well the new building codes had been

The Sichuan earthquake uncovered issues regarding construction.

enforced. Some scientists believed the quake was triggered by the construction of a reservoir near a geologic fault line. They suspected that the weight of 320 million short tons (290,299,116 t) of water may have caused the quake.

Haiti, 2010

In 2010, Haiti received massive damage and loss of life as a result of an earthquake. Haiti is a small nation in the Caribbean that shares the island of Hispaniola with the Dominican Republic. Haiti had been hit by hurricanes and other tropical storms as recently as 2008, but a major earthquake had not struck the region since 1770. Then, on January 12, 2010, a magnitude 7.0 quake hit near Port-au-Prince, the capital. Aftershocks, some with magnitudes greater than 5.0, registered for weeks.

Haiti's most populated areas were almost completely destroyed. Tens of thousands of people were killed immediately, many as a result of poorly constructed buildings falling on them. Thousands were injured and had to wait for treatment because hospitals suffered severe damage.

Naming Hurricanes

The practice of naming hurricanes developed to make communications and storm tracking easier. Originally, in the West Indies, hurricanes were named after the particular saint's day on which the storm occurred, such as Hurricane San Felipe in Puerto Rico on September 13, 1876. This system became cumbersome when another hurricane occurred on the same day in 1928. It was named Hurricane San Felipe the Second. Later, hurricanes were named after their latitude and longitude positions, which was subject to error and difficult to remember.

The United States began naming storms officially in 1953. Only female names were used until 1978. The names come from the World Meteorological Organization, which generated six lists of names drawn from different cultures. Hurricanes in the Atlantic Ocean can have English, French, or Spanish names because these are primary languages used in areas bordering the Atlantic. A storm is named when it has a counterclockwise rotation of winds greater than 39 miles per hour (63 km/h). Storms are given names starting with *A* and progressing through the alphabet, alternating male and female names: *Q, U,* and *Z* are not used because few names begin with those letters. Names associated with storms that caused large scale destruction and numerous deaths are not reused.

Countless others were trapped alive in collapsed buildings. More than 1 million Haitians were left homeless, without shelter, water, and electricity.

The earthquake was perhaps not as big as some others, but the devastation was massive. Haiti was destroyed at every level—even the president lost his home. The nation's extreme poverty, poor infrastructure, and lack of disaster preparedness and response had particularly devastating results.

Scientists Warned of Possible Danger

The January 2010 earthquake in Haiti was not a surprise to everyone. In March 2008, five scientists representing five universities published a paper warning of the possible danger. They wrote, "Such studies should be considered high priority in Jamaica, Haiti and the Dominican Republic given the seismic hazards posed by the fault."[2]

PAKISTAN, 2010

Haiti was not the only nation to experience disaster in 2010. The worst flooding in 80 years struck Pakistan's Punjab and Sindh provinces in August, destroying crops and homes. The Indus River and Chenab River flooded the surrounding land. Some 250,000 residents were forced to evacuate as waters rose. As the disaster spread, the divide between those with money and those without became more and more apparent, just as it had in New Orleans when Hurricane Katrina struck. Those with transportation evacuated the area immediately. Others escaped by hiring trucks.

However, the 100,000 residents without money or transportation were left behind to fend for themselves. Many built makeshift shelters on higher ground and watched as their permanent homes were washed away. While the government supplied food to many residents, its ability to help all of the victims was limited. More than 1,600 people died from the disaster and more than 20 million people were affected.

Each of these recent events, though devastating, provided valuable information about disaster prediction, preparedness, response, and recovery. Researchers continue to better their understanding of the geologic and meteorologic forces that shape the planet and affect individuals and their communities. Still, scientists are able to predict only some events and with little advance warning.

Flood survivors in Pakistan stand in line for drinking water
in September 2010.

Natural disasters come in two types and many forms.

PREDICTION

Natural disasters can be divided into two categories: geologic and meteorologic. Earth's geologic processes cause devastating natural disasters that are often difficult to predict. These include earthquakes, volcanoes, and tsunamis.

Natural disasters that occur as a result of meteorologic forces are the most common and are often the easiest to predict. These include hurricanes, tornadoes, floods, and snow and ice storms.

EARTHQUAKES

Earth's crust, or its land, is the planet's thin outer layer. It floats on Earth's mantle, a semi-molten layer surrounding Earth's core. The crust is comprised of several plates that support the continents. Approximately 250 million years ago, all of Earth's continents were a single landmass known as Pangaea, which broke apart. The plates continue to move at rates of two to four inches (5 to 10 cm) per year.

The plates ram into each other, pull apart, and create pressure on the seams where they touch. When enough strain builds, these plates may slip or lurch, resulting

Ring of Fire

Many geologic disasters occur along the Ring of Fire. The most volcanically active region in the world, the Ring of Fire lies along the Pacific Rim. This region includes three-fourths of the world's volcanoes. The ring starts along the western coast of South America, moves up along the Central American and Mexican coast, and then along the Pacific Northwestern coast of North America. The top of the ring stretches along Alaska's Aleutian Islands and around Russia's Kamchatka Peninsula. It then moves down through Japan and continues to New Zealand.

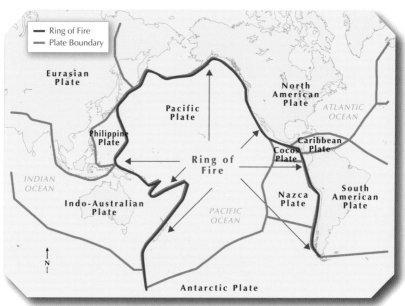

The Ring of Fire is a hotbed of geologic activity.

in earthquakes. Most earthquakes occur where the plates meet, areas called fault lines. Earthquakes also occur at cracks in Earth's surface.

Estimating the likelihood of an earthquake depends on monitoring of geologic faults for strain and looking at the frequency of past earthquakes for that particular area. According to the US Geological Survey,

> When plate movements build the strain in rocks to a critical level, like pulling a rubber band too tight, the rocks will

suddenly break and slip to a new position. Scientists measure how much strain accumulates along a fault segment each year, how much time has passed since the last earthquake along the segment, and how much strain was released in the last earthquake. This information is then used to calculate the time required for the accumulating strain to build to a level that results in an earthquake.[1]

Scientists want to one day be able to predict earthquakes with enough warning to enable people in a particular area to prepare. At present, the best they can do is provide a long-term warning that a major earthquake could occur and to recommend earthquake-resistant construction in those areas.

Volcanoes

Volcanoes occur where plates are meeting and pulling apart, or converging and diverging. Friction and heat melt the edges of these plates and create places where liquid rock, or magma, can rise to the surface, melting more of the crust as it goes. As this magma collects near the surface, pressure builds until the earth breaks open and the magma is expelled. Magma can be thin and runny, which creates bright orange lava that flows in rivers, or it can be thick, trapping vapors and gases that bubble to the surface and explode into clouds of stone and ash. The vapors can be lethal for humans to breathe, and, as Krakatau demonstrated, can block the sun and affect weather. Great destruction also occurs as hot lava spreads across land, obliterating everything in its path.

Scientists can generally tell if a volcano is active—meaning it has the potential to erupt within the next decade, century, or even longer. They assess a volcano's status by monitoring earthquake activity around its base. They also keep track of a volcano's changing shape, which could indicate increasing pressure in the magma below it. A third method is to analyze the gases coming out of the volcano. Even with these assessments, scientists are only occasionally able to make precise predictions to warn nearby residents that an eruption is imminent.

The Danger of Dormancy

Volcanoes are also dangerous because they may remain dormant for long periods of time between eruptions. This encourages people to build in their vicinity, which makes people even more vulnerable when these volcanoes erupt again. In addition to spewing ash, lava, and gases, they can spark landslides, mudslides, and fires.

Tsunamis

A tsunami, or tidal wave, is a type of disaster that can result from an earthquake or volcanic eruption, events that disturb ocean waters. Waves increase in height as they head toward land, just as a rock thrown into a pond creates ripples that spread from the point where the rock broke the surface of the water.

Because tsunamis are linked to earthquakes and volcanic eruptions, officials can issue a tsunami warning based on the location of the initial incident. This warning will indicate the possibility for a tidal wave and where the wave could land. But warnings are issued only just before tsunamis occur. Tsunamis do have warning signs. Sometimes, the ocean may seem to bubble. Other times, the water may pull away from the shore and expose large areas of sand before huge walls of water sweep in from enormous waves, just as occurred in 2004 during the Indian Ocean tsunami.

The National Oceanographic and Atmospheric Administration (NOAA) monitors all seismic activity. When a sizeable earthquake takes place around the globe, these centers locate the epicenter and estimate its size. They then send bulletins to the countries that belong to the International Tsunami Warning System for the Pacific Ocean. Scientists use computer simulations and models to attempt to determine whether a tsunami has been generated and what its path might be.

But not every seismic event triggers a tsunami. Scientists also rely on a network of instruments located in the ocean itself, as well as tide gauges placed on land, to monitor sea level and alert scientists of sudden rises in water level.

Hurricanes

Hurricanes may go by other names, depending on the part of the world in which they occur. Whether they are called hurricanes, cyclones, or typhoons, these are the biggest storms on Earth. A hurricane storm system may be as large as 500 miles (805 km) from one side of its signature swirling circular shape to the other. It may also generate an amazing amount of energy, sometimes equal to 200 times the capacity of the entire world's electric generation systems in a day.

Hurricanes are all born in tropical waters near the equator. And while all hurricanes move, many break up without reaching land. Others, however,

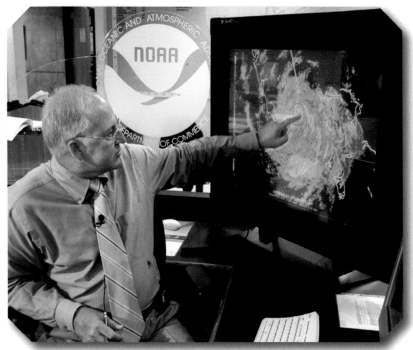

In August 2005, National Hurricane Center Director Max Mayfield tracked Hurricane Katrina via computer.

move, grow, and make landfall, as was the case with Hurricane Katrina in 2005. While most hurricanes quickly lose strength over land, their high winds and heavy rain can still inflict heavy damage before dissipating. Also destructive are the extremely high ocean waves that are pushed inland and storm surge flooding.

In the past, hurricanes would strike almost without warning, as forecasters depended only on observations of the sky and perhaps reports from ships at sea. Scientists do not yet understand all the factors that result in the formation of a hurricane. However, they have a better understanding of the life cycle of a hurricane and are able to watch tropical storms as they form near the equator.

NOAA maintains national and central-Pacific hurricane centers. In addition to operating local National Weather Service offices across the country, NOAA monitors the weather in the tropics and looks for storms. Using a variety of technology, NOAA can now forecast hurricanes five days in advance. This enables communities in the path of the storm to prepare. It also allows time for US Navy ships and other vessels to be moved out of the storm's path.

Tornadoes

A tornado, or twister, is a massive column of spinning winds that drops from a cloud and moves across land. Tornadoes have the fastest and strongest winds of any kind of storm—much faster than the winds associated with hurricanes. Scientists have clocked tornado wind speeds at 318 miles per hour (512 km/h). With this much force, a tornado is capable of lifting buildings off their foundations,

Tornadoes drop from the sky, often with little or no warning, which makes preparing for these natural disasters difficult.

tearing roofs off buildings, or flattening them completely. It can sweep entire towns clean, destroying every structure in its path.

A tornado begins as a funnel cloud—a cloud shaped like a funnel—hanging below the storm. Once the funnel cloud touches ground, it becomes a tornado. Tornadoes may be white or gray, but as they touch the ground and pull up soil, they change depending on the color of the dirt they pick up. Tornadoes also pick up rocks, bicycles, and other objects in their paths.

Tornado Alley

Tornado Alley is a name for the area of the United States where tornadoes are most likely to occur. This area includes northern Texas, Oklahoma, Kansas, the Ohio Valley, the Tennessee Valley, and the lower Mississippi Valley. In these areas, stricter building codes may call for structures that are more resistant to tornadoes, including stronger roofs and better connections between buildings and their foundations. More people may have storm shelters. Municipal areas may also have tornado warning sirens in place.

Tornadoes are even more difficult to predict than hurricanes, because they occur with less warning and similar weather patterns may not always produce tornadoes. In addition, the weather conditions that spawn tornadoes may develop on a small, localized scale, between weather stations.

One tool for predicting tornadoes is a set of specific weather conditions. The presence of thunderstorms is a vital clue, especially a supercell storm, which often visibly spins and twists at its core. This kind of storm produces the strongest tornadoes. Forecasters rely on technology and local weather spotters, people who monitor the skies and inform them of any funnel clouds or tornadoes in their areas. Still, sometimes a storm with every characteristic that might make it ripe for tornadoes does not produce one. This makes it difficult for forecasters to know when to warn the public. John Hart of the Storm Prediction Center in Norman, Oklahoma, explained:

The tornado is one of the most powerful, yet elusive, forces on Earth. Despite decades of research, we are still not able to predict the actual path of a tornado.[2]

FLOODS AND DROUGHTS

Floods and droughts are natural disasters at the extremes in terms of water. Floods occur when any kind of water, such as lakes and rivers, breaks its boundaries. Floods can be generated by the water from a hurricane, a monsoon, a long-lasting and slow-moving thunderstorm, snow melt, or a shifting ocean current. They are capable of sweeping away buildings and destroying roads and farmland. The effects of flooding are usually increased because people often build homes and businesses in floodplains, places near bodies of water known to have flooded in the past. Floodwaters can also contaminate freshwater supplies.

Droughts, on the other hand, occur when there is a lack of water, because of heat waves or limited

Fire Tornadoes

If the right conditions exist, a fire tornado can develop. It is a rare occurrence caused by brush fires and strong winds. When it does happen, a column of fire can stretch 30 to 200 feet (9 to 61 m) from the ground into the air. A fire tornado was filmed on August 25, 2010, in Aracatuba, Brazil. It resulted when several months of drought and dry winds combined with brush fires.

rainfall or both. Vegetation and crops dry up and die. Not only do crops, people, and animals suffer from a lack of water, but the dry landscape may also lead to wildfires that can destroy forests and adjacent communities.

Floods are forecasted using weather radar and computer models that show where floodwaters are most likely to flow. Prediction takes into account the atmosphere as well as the kind of soil on which the rain is falling. Predicting the severity of floods that result from breached dams or bodies of water, or those

---

Measuring Destruction

Some types of natural disasters have their own measurement system. This allows scientists to categorize the size or intensity of the disaster. It also allows them to make inferences about the circumstances that may have created a particular event's strength and compare it to previous and future events.

Hurricanes are measured using the Saffir-Simpson Hurricane Wind Scale, which categorizes them from 1 to 5 according to wind speed, with 5 being the worst. Tornadoes are measured according to the Enhanced Fujita (EF) Scale, which uses a scale of EF-0 to EF-5 based on damage—according to a specific Degree of Damage scale—and estimated wind speed. An EF-1 tornado may overturn cars or peel the surface of a roof, while an EF-5 tornado will lift houses off their foundations and carry them through the air for long distances. Earthquakes are measured using the Richter scale, which records the seismic waves generated by the quake on a scale of whole numbers and decimal fractions, with no upper limit. A 2.0 earthquake will not usually be felt by the average person, a 4.5 quake will register on most seismographs around the world, and an extremely devastating earthquake might be an 8.0.

that accompany storm surges, may not be possible. Floods in areas that rarely experience them may also take residents by surprise.

Predicting droughts is more challenging. Scientists examine how meteorologic events interact to create weather patterns and what these patterns might mean for a particular region's weather. While researchers continue to build their understanding of weather, they generally are unable to predict droughts more than one month in advance, which leaves scientists to monitor droughts more than predict them.

DEADLY ICE AND SNOW

Winter storms such as ice storms and blizzards can be just as deadly as hurricanes and tornadoes. These storms are created by frozen precipitation. These cold weather events may disrupt power, often leaving thousands of people without electricity for days. Travel can also be hazardous, making it difficult to travel in emergency situations.

Avalanches are another type of snow disaster that can be deadly. In the case of an avalanche, the effects of snow are delayed. Massive amounts of accumulated snowfall become dislodged from a mountainside, sending a wave of ice and snow down the slopes. Avalanches can smother people and buildings with tons of snow. They can also carry damaging rocks and fallen trees down the mountainside.

Using radar and satellite imagery, as well as monitoring moisture in the air, forecasters can usually warn an area to expect a storm. However, forecasters are not always able to accurately estimate how much precipitation will fall or whether it will be heavy snow or ice, which might result in widespread damage and power outages.

Areas vulnerable to avalanches can be identified based on snowpack and whether they have treeless slopes and overhangs. This allows authorities to post warnings or even close areas where avalanches would most likely occur.

Not every natural disaster can be successfully predicted. But some sort of warning about an impending event can make all the difference in saving lives and property. This is especially so when preparations are already in place for potential disasters.

Researchers use weather balloons to record meteorologic information.

The earthquake that devastated Haiti in 2010 showed the effects of natural disasters on impoverished areas and the importance of international relief.

PREPARATION

Scientists have become better at predicting disasters, or at least identifying the signs that might indicate one is imminent. Close monitoring and modern weather forecasting have not been able to prevent major natural disasters from having devastating effects in the twenty-first century. However, preparation can dramatically limit the loss caused by natural disasters.

MITIGATION, PREPAREDNESS, RESPONSE, RECOVERY

To successfully prepare for any disaster, communities must focus on four basic steps of emergency management: mitigation, preparedness, response, and recovery. Mitigation means lessening the impact disasters have on people and property. It involves modifying building codes to avoid construction in high-risk areas such as floodplains, engineering buildings to withstand high winds or earthquake tremors, or avoiding flat-roofed structures in areas that receive heavy snowfall.

Preparedness is being ready to respond to emergencies in the event of a disaster. Those responsible for preparedness are usually government agencies, community and civic groups, facilities such as hospitals and schools, and emergency responders. Preparedness involves learning what types of natural disasters may strike and making sure sufficient equipment and supplies are on hand to cope with an emergency situation. It may also involve setting up evacuation routes, designating shelters, and distributing information about evacuation procedures and other emergency measures.

The response portion of emergency management occurs when well-trained and well-equipped personnel step into action to address the disaster. It requires a plan for dealing with victims who may be homeless or injured as well as for controlling looting.

Finally, recovery is the process of returning to normal life as soon as possible. It may involve salvage or demolition of damaged structures; repairing infrastructures such as roads, communication facilities, and water and sewer services; and helping businesses reopen.

Specific Preparations

Each kind of disaster requires specific preparation, and people who live in areas prone to certain types of disasters should make every effort to be prepared for them. In hurricane areas such as coastal Florida or the Gulf Coast, homes can be equipped with hurricane shutters to protect windows from being broken by high winds. Roofs and doors should be reinforced to withstand high winds.

*Sandbags were placed in front of a door
in preparation for flooding.*

Emergency kits with food, water, first-aid supplies, a cell phone, and a battery radio are important to keep on hand, and cars should have a full tank of gas in the event of a forced evacuation.

Those who live in areas where tornadoes are frequent need to have a safe place to take cover if one strikes. This includes a storm cellar, basement, or interior room without windows.

Flooding can be difficult to prepare for, but the best preparation is to construct homes on higher ground and not on floodplains or riverbanks. Water-resistant construction materials are ideal. Homeowners should have an emergency kit and a supply of food and water on hand at all times.

Structures built in earthquake zones need to be braced and well-anchored. Some are built on special foundations that allow the building to move without collapsing. In many earthquake zones, building codes mandate earthquake-resistant building methods. In the event of an actual quake, residents need to know how to find the safest place in their homes and go into duck and cover, a practice where they crouch under a large piece of furniture and cover their heads for protection from falling debris.

Volcanic eruptions and tsunamis are more difficult to plan for and rely mostly on an effective means of communication to warn the public of

Building for Earthquakes

Buildings in earthquake-prone areas can be constructed so as to limit the earthquake damage. Structures should not be built on land that might liquefy, such as reclaimed swampland or sand. Buildings constructed of flexible materials, such as wood or steel, will move with the quake without collapsing, while unreinforced masonry or concrete will crack. Building joints need to be reinforced to survive movement, and trusses can help support a building while allowing it to flex. Ground isolators isolate a building's foundation from the rest of the structure, allowing it to move with the ground independently from the rest of the structure.

Filipino students covered their heads with boxes and books during an earthquake drill. The event was part of government efforts in disaster preparedness and awareness among local agencies and the public.

the impending disaster. Clearly marked evacuation routes are vital to enable people to find the fastest way out of the danger zone.

Complete preparation is not possible, but having procedures and systems in place before a disaster strikes can make a dramatic difference in loss of life and destruction of property. Lack of preparedness can result in terrible consequences, as was the case with Hurricane Katrina and the earthquake in Haiti.

A Failure to Prepare: New Orleans

After Hurricane Georges hit the Gulf Coast in 1998, Louisiana state officials asked for the federal government to help develop plans in the event that a major hurricane should strike New Orleans. Four years later, in 2002, an article in the *Institute of Transportation Engineers Journal* noted that New Orleans's evacuation plans were inadequate. The article noted "a lack of access to transportation (it is estimated that about 200,000 to 300,000 people do not have access to reliable personal transportation), an unwillingness to leave homes and property (estimated to be at least 100,000 people) and a lack of outbound roadway capacity."[1]

These inadequacies, and others, were highlighted in 2005 when Hurricane Katrina struck the city. In addition to evacuation routes that were too limited and too

Earthquake Drills

Because of the frequency of earthquakes in Japan, children there take part in earthquake drills at their schools once a month. They are taught to get under their desks head first and hold onto the legs of the desk until the quake's movement stops. Next, the teacher leads them outside, making sure every student is accounted for. Sometimes, they practice earthquake drills in a special room that shakes, simulating a quake. Children in classrooms on the second floor of their schools may practice using special emergency chutes to quickly carry them to ground level.

congested, the city used a major evacuation site—the Superdome—that was too close to the disaster and lost power and water just as the rest of the city did. In addition, a mandatory evacuation order was not enforced. People were left behind. Some lost their lives; some resorted to looting. There was a failure to anticipate the city's needs when it came to an evacuation plan, which left people behind who were not able or could not afford to escape. New Orleans officials, especially

Sinkholes

On June 2, 2010, a hole measuring 66 feet (20 m) wide and 100 feet (30 m) deep appeared on a street in Guatemala City, Guatemala. An intersection disappeared and several buildings were destroyed. There had been intense rainfall in the months prior to the event, but residents had complained of deep rumblings and sinking land in the area since 2005. Some scientists believe leaking sewer pipes may have contributed to the erosion underground. A similar event occurred in the city in 2007.

This phenomenon is known as a sinkhole. It can happen suddenly or gradually. Sudden, or collapse, sinkholes can be disastrous. They produce deep craters with steep sides. Gradual, or subsidence, sinkholes occur less dramatically. As they slowly sink, soil and sand settle in the empty space, creating a hole with gradually sloping sides.

Sinkholes are caused when groundwater flows through rock beneath the ground's surface. The rock is a kind that can be easily dissolved, such as limestone or salt deposits. As water washes away the rock, an open cavern is created below ground. If the water drains from the cavern, its roof is no longer supported, or the weight above ground can become too much for the roof to take. That is when the cavern roof collapses, exposing a sometimes enormous hole in the ground.

the police, also blamed inept or incomplete commands from city and government officials. There was a lack of clear communication about who had survived the storm and where to get information on where to go and what to do.

These and other problems combined to make the effects of Hurricane Katrina much worse than they might have been with proper planning. The government report *Hurricane Katrina: A Nation Still Unprepared* assessed what happened:

> *Ineffective leadership, poor advance planning, and an unwillingness to devote sufficient resources to emergency management over the long term doomed them to fail when Katrina struck. Despite the understanding of the Gulf Coast's particular vulnerability to hurricane devastation, officials braced for Katrina with full awareness of critical deficiencies in their plans and gaping*

Watches and Warnings

The National Weather Service uses a system of watches and warnings to inform the public of impending weather situations. A watch means conditions are right for a weather event to take place and people need to be alert to weather conditions by tuning into a radio or television station and being ready to act by taking shelter or evacuating. A warning indicates dangerous weather is now threatening the area and the public needs to take immediate action. The National Weather Service cannot stop a natural disaster from occurring, but its warnings can lessen human loss.

holes in their resources. While Katrina's destructive force could not be denied, state and local officials did not marshal enough of the resources at their disposal.[2]

While it is impossible to say how many lives and how much money in damages might have been saved with proper planning for Hurricane Katrina, experts do agree that more people would have survived if they had been able—or had been forced—to evacuate the city.

And perhaps damage from flooding could have been reduced if the levees surrounding the city had been better maintained. The levees had been modified to withstand the force of a Category 3 hurricane, but when Katrina hit, it was closer to a Category 4 storm. Also, the city depended on a system of pumps to push water uphill and away from the city, back into Lake Pontchartrain and the Mississippi River. These pumps, which ran on electricity, ceased to operate when power was lost.

MUNICH RE'S REPORT

Hurricane Katrina is only one example of how a lack of preparation and emergency planning can make a tremendous difference in lives lost and property damaged as the result of a natural disaster. But it is an example of a nation with the resources to prepare properly.

But lack of preparation is not always the result of poor planning. Sometimes, disaster preparation suffers because resources simply do not exist. Developing nations cannot mitigate or prepare thoroughly. Munich Re is an international insurance company that reviews natural disasters annually. In its review of 2003, Munich Re noted an earthquake in Bam, Iran, that killed 40,000. Most of the fatalities were the result of poorly designed housing that could not withstand a major tremor. Munich Re reported, "Traditional buildings of mud brick and heavy roofing are particularly unsafe when earthquakes strike."[3]

Planning and preparation are important for dealing with natural disasters, regardless of a nation's wealth. But even the best planning will not keep damage and death from occurring. It is important that areas hit by natural disasters are also able to respond to the aftereffects, and how they do this can make a difference in the ongoing health and recovery of their community.

*A father and son board up the windows of their house
in preparation for a hurricane.*

Rescue teams aid victims in a community mock disaster drill.

RESPONSE

A natural disaster has taken place, and even with prediction and preparation, there has been loss of life, injury, and damage to property. What happens next is critical. Ideally, the community will have some sort of system for dealing with the effects of the disaster, but responding to a natural disaster goes beyond the scope of the local community and its government.

A National Response Framework

The Federal Emergency Management Agency (FEMA), which is part of the Department of Homeland Security, has a framework for dealing with disasters and other emergencies in the United States. The National Response Framework spells out a comprehensive approach for responding to these events. It clearly designates roles and structures, which organizes how a disaster is dealt with on the local, state, and national levels.

The framework notes that the local chief official or chief executive officer—a mayor or city manager—is responsible for guiding response and recovery. Any disaster with the potential for long-term effects in the areas of public health, economy, environment, and crime, requires a coordinated response from public officials, business owners, and other community leaders.

At the state level, the governor is responsible for safety and public welfare and for coordinating state-level response. At the federal level, the response is meant to be flexible and adaptable to the specific type of emergency taking place. The president leads the response efforts, with advice from the Homeland Security Council, the National Security Council, and FEMA's administrator. The president can officially declare a major disaster or state of emergency; however, a presidential declaration is not required to gain federal assistance.

Nongovernment agencies also step in to help provide shelter, emergency food supplies, and counseling for disaster victims. These groups include the American Red Cross, National Voluntary Organizations Active in Disaster, and other volunteers and donors.

Dealing with Disaster

There are many issues to deal with in the aftermath of a natural disaster. First and foremost, survivors must be rescued and treated for any injuries. They will also need a safe place to stay, food, water, and other necessities. Fatalities must be dealt with as well, especially since decomposing bodies can cause illness. Lists must be compiled of survivors and the dead, to enable others to locate family members.

Personal safety is another critical concern. This includes preventing illness and maintaining good mental health after a disaster. Special consideration must be given to pregnant women and people with chronic health issues as well as dealing with pets, creating and maintaining evacuation centers and services for evacuees, and coordinating and housing emergency response workers.

Long-term responses include providing additional permanent shelters for people who have lost their homes, rebuilding roads and sewage and water systems,

Tsunami Relief

The 2004 tsunami that swept across the Indian Ocean was an example of a natural disaster that triggered relief response from all over the world. Because of the Internet and television, people around the world could view the tsunami's devastation almost immediately, and individuals and countries alike pledged relief money in the billions of dollars.

The International Red Cross and Red Crescent Societies and other humanitarian groups rushed to the area to assist with medical help, shelter, food, identifying the missing and the dead, and reuniting survivors—especially children—with their families. In the first seven weeks, the organization Doctors Without Borders/Médecins Sans Frontières sent 2,500 workers and 1,200 short tons (1,089 t) of relief supplies. The charity CARE delivered food, water-purification packets, and medical supplies. However, the relief effort did not always proceed smoothly. Deliveries were delayed because of damage to roads and airports and bureaucracy that required donations to pass through customs, leaving them on airport runways for days before they could be sent to where they were needed. But overall, the relief efforts were some of the biggest outpourings of global assistance in history.

Signs of Disaster

After Hurricane Katrina devastated New Orleans, rescuers had the grim task of going through neighborhoods and looking for survivors, dead bodies, and hazards such as gas leaks. They used a system of marking houses with spray paint to indicate when they were searched, by what team, and if any hazards or dead bodies were found.

restoring power, and reopening businesses, schools, and hospitals. These tasks may take months or even years to accomplish.

A Case Study in Response: New Orleans

Hurricane Katrina was an example of a disaster that should have been handled according to the National Response Framework. But failures in communication hampered the response to Katrina. In the years since the hurricane, there has been a great deal of discussion and blame assigned for some of the mistakes that happened in New Orleans in 2005. A report from a congressional committee examining the aftermath of Katrina called the response "a litany of mistakes, misjudgments, lapses and absurdities."[1]

Miscommunication was the greatest impediment to evacuating people from New Orleans both as the hurricane approached and after it struck. Confusion existed as to who was in charge and what resources had to be provided and when. Equipment and communications in the city were hampered by lack of power and dependable communication systems, leaving National Guard troops to literally run messages back and forth in person because they lacked proper equipment. Critics claimed that no one at the top level of the government took charge of the situation, and lack of communication and collaboration between all levels hampered the handling of the crisis. Others felt that FEMA had been largely ignored by the Department of Homeland Security because the country was more focused on terrorism than disaster preparedness after the events of September 11, 2001. Also, many of the jobs within FEMA were unfilled, leaving the department understaffed and inexperienced.

An example of the failure of agencies and the government to communicate took place on the morning of August 31, 2005, roughly 48 hours after the hurricane struck. According to Angie Marek in an article in *U.S. News and World Report*:

Disaster Declarations

When the US president declares a disaster or national emergency in an area hit by a natural disaster, it is because the federal government has determined that the damage and recovery costs in that area are beyond the resources of the community or state. Once the declaration is official, the federal government will offer money and direct services, including loans, to individuals and businesses whose property was damaged by the disaster.

A Red Cross volunteer comforted a Hurricane Katrina victim in 2005.

[FEMA officials] and the Louisiana National Guard were prepared to evacuate the wretched men, women and children huddling in the Superdome, using Chinook and Black Hawk helicopters. They had worked through the night finalizing the plan, but just hours before they were set to begin, they were told to stop. The Guard had learned that active-duty [US Army] troops . . . were planning to airlift the evacuees out of the dome. [Though] Louisiana Gov. Kathleen Babineaux Blanco had requested [the army's] help; neither thought to tell FEMA about the plan. The result: The miserable people in the dome would have to wait an additional 24 hours before the evacuation began. [2]

This was just one instance of miscommunication and the failure of agencies to work together in addressing the problems that resulted from Katrina.

Hurricane Katrina highlighted holes and weaknesses in the ability of local, state, and federal governments and agencies to respond rapidly and efficiently to a natural disaster in the United States. Several reports by congressional committees have analyzed Katrina and what went wrong, so they can make recommendations for changes in agencies and response plans to ensure that a future disaster will be dealt with more efficiently and effectively.

THE IMPORTANCE OF INTERNATIONAL AID

FEMA and other US organizations responded to the disaster in New Orleans. But some nations, especially developing ones, require considerable support from international organizations and other nations to survive a disaster. Haiti is one example.

The Response Process

According to the National Response Framework, responding to a natural disaster is a four-part process. First, authorities must gain an overall awareness of the situation. Next, key resources and capabilities must be activated and deployed. Then, response to the disaster must be coordinated among local, state, and national authorities. Finally, once the situation is under control, responding agencies will be demobilized as necessary.

FEMA Trailers

FEMA offers temporary trailers or manufactured housing to disaster victims. These can be quickly brought to a disaster area to provide housing for people who have lost their homes or whose homes are uninhabitable. The trailers are intended to provide long-term shelter to replace temporary housing such as tents. Sometimes, residents live in them for years. FEMA trailers are the property of the US government and meant to be returned after use, though some residents eventually purchase the trailers from FEMA at reduced prices.

The earthquake that struck Haiti in early 2010 devastated the nation. Help was needed to recover the trapped, treat the injured, provide temporary shelter for the homeless, supply food and clean water, and clean up the rubble, which included bodies of thousands of people. Nations, organizations, and individuals worldwide quickly donated a variety of resources, including medical teams and supplies, search-and-rescue teams, food, clothing, and money. The day after the earthquake, the United Nations (UN) promised $10 million to Haiti. UN Secretary-General Ban Ki-moon said of the disaster, "It is a tragedy for Haiti, for the Haitian people and for the United Nations."[3]

For nations such as Haiti, international aid is critical to help a disaster-stricken area respond to a tragedy. For many areas affected by natural disasters, extensive resources—especially money—will also be needed to address recovery.

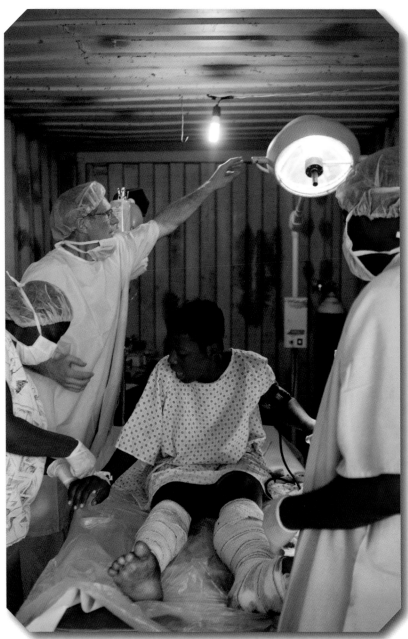

Haitians were treated by members of Doctors Without Borders/
Médecins Sans Frontières at a makeshift clinic in January 2010.

German Red Cross members and volunteers loaded relief aid for Pakistan into an airplane in Berlin, Germany, in August 2010.

RECOVERY

When disaster strikes, response focuses on victims' immediate needs, such as food, water, shelter, and safety. Different levels of response will be needed to address the two types of effects of the disaster: short-term and long-term.

Short-Term Recovery

Natural disasters can cause tremendous destruction that affects victims in a variety of ways. Many victims suffer the loss of the basic resources required for living, including shelter, food, and water. For some, there is the more personal loss of mementos. Some victims must recover from physical injuries; some must deal with mental and emotional issues that happen from the pure shock of the event. Financial challenges occur when businesses are destroyed, leaving business owners and their employees without much-needed income.

Many of these issues are often addressed immediately, in short-term recovery, in the form of assistance from the government and organizations such as the Red Cross. Mental health professionals can assist in dealing with the loss and shock caused by the disaster. And insurance can provide money to replace items lost.

Long-Term Recovery

Long-term recovery takes into account the long-term needs of victims, including their community and, when necessary, their nation. Long-term recovery may include challenges faced in short-

term recovery. Houses and other buildings may
need to be repaired or rebuilt. In the case of Haiti,
these structures will have to be constructed to
better withstand future earthquakes and tropical
storms and hurricanes. And employment and
businesses may take months or years to return to
an area damaged by a natural disaster. Parts of an
area's infrastructure, such as roads, might need
rebuilding. Sometimes, education must be addressed
when schools are destroyed. Loss of schools and
education opportunities could affect a nation for
years by leaving its youth without
the knowledge and skills needed to
take on important professional and
leadership roles.

In the case of Haiti, some
children moved to the United States
for better resources, including
education. While this migration
is good for the children in terms
of getting basic needs met, it is a
challenging situation because families
are separated. This was also the case
with New Orleans residents who were
moved elsewhere, such as to Texas,

Helping the Animals

Hurricane Katrina affected
all residents of New
Orleans, including its pets.
More than 250,000 pets
were stranded in the city
after the storm. In many
cases, owners left their pets
behind, leaving them food
and water with the belief
they would return in a few
days. Veterinarians and
members of animal res-
cue organizations scoured
flooded areas of the city
for abandoned animals,
many of which were
dehydrated, starving, and
scared without the care of
their owners.

as part of the rescue and recovery efforts. While family members were given safe shelter and other resources, families were sometimes separated, which brought a new stress to victims. And those who were relocated had to rebuild their lives, which included establishing a home and possibly finding a job, and creating or becoming part of a new community.

Recovery is broad and varied. It must address issues related to physical and psychological health, economics, and infrastructure. Some issues may be adequately addressed in a matter of months. In other instances, recovery may take years.

International Red Cross and Red Crescent Societies

The idea for the Red Cross developed in the mind of a Swiss man in 1859. Henry Dunant saw the results of a battle between Italian and Austrian armies. Approximately 40,000 soldiers were dead or dying. Medical attention was sorely needed. Dunant called locals into action, charging them with caring for soldiers. He called upon greater forces to create national relief societies to help casualties of war:

Would there not be some means, during a period of peace and calm, of forming relief societies whose object would be to have the wounded cared for in time of war by enthusiastic, devoted volunteers, fully qualified for the task?[1]

Five nations founded relief societies: Britain, France, Italy, Japan, and the United States. As of 2010, there were 186 recognized societies. The International Federation of Red Cross and Red Crescent Societies was founded in 1919, in the aftermath of World War I (1914–1918), when many Europeans needed assistance. Coordinating efforts across Red Cross Societies was needed.

FIVE YEARS AFTER KATRINA

On August 29, 2010, many reflected on the aftermath of Hurricane Katrina as they marked its fifth anniversary. Eighty percent of New Orleans's former population lives in the city. Many areas have been rebuilt and construction continues, but there are still pockets of deserted and destroyed neighborhoods in the city. In 2009, 40,000 families were still living in FEMA trailers, housing intended as a temporary solution. According to Housing and Urban Development Secretary Shaun Donovan, by August 2010, 98 percent of those families had moved out of the trailers and into permanent housing.

In Waveland, Mississippi, Katrina wiped out all businesses and nearly all homes in the town. The city used $100 million in federal aid to rebuild the town's schools, roads, parks, and utilities. Approximately 65 percent of businesses and residents have returned to the city.

Rebuilding from Katrina has been slow, though, as aid has been stuck in federal bureaucracy. FEMA authorized $8.9 billion. While city officials fight for their claims to the aid, rebuilding projects are stalled. It took three years for a fire station to be

Five years after Hurricane Katrina, destruction in New Orleans was still evident.

rebuilt in Grand Isle, Louisiana. Finally, the $3 million was granted and the fire station opened in July 2010. Funds are still needed to repair schools, hospitals, roads, and other community needs in the damaged areas.

Haiti Follow-up

Recovery in Haiti has been slow. Six months after the earthquake, many people still lived in tents with barely any possessions. Nearly 1.5 million people were left homeless by the earthquake. In July 2010, only 28,000 had been moved into

permanent housing. Crime was also on the rise.
While donations of money and materials have been
pledged, decisions have not been made on how to
use the donations. Building materials sit in Haiti's
customs for weeks. Critics say Haiti's president,
René Préval, has not made the critical decisions
needed to make the rebuilding process progress.

The Interim Haiti Recovery Commission was
created to plan and manage long-term rebuilding
projects. It has donations to work
with, but the agency's work has
been slow as well. Haitians are still
suffering from the earthquake's
devastation. They have been patient,
but as 2010 came to a close, a
clear strategy for Haiti's recovery
still needed to be developed and
communicated to the nation's
waiting citizens. A challenge remains,
however, in that Haiti, while having
received considerable support from
the rest of world, remains a nation
steeped in poverty.

Haiti: A Worsening Situation

As relief descended on Haiti to help the nation respond to the earthquake that struck in January 2010, long-term concerns were expressed about disease. Water was limited and polluted and human waste littered the streets.

These concerns were realized later that year, in October, when there was an outbreak of cholera. Cholera can cause severe diarrhea and vomiting, which can result in dehydration. The disease can be fatal and had resulted in more than 1,000 deaths in Haiti by mid-November.

In November 2010, people in Haiti walked in rain brought by Hurricane
Tomas at a camp for people displaced by the January earthquake.

Children sat in a flooded tent after Hurricane Tomas passed over Haiti in November 2010.

WHEN RESOURCES ARE LIMITED

*P*rediction, preparation, response, and recovery are designed with the optimal resources and results in mind. However, optimal is often not reality. This is especially so in areas where poverty exists.

Disasters are linked to poverty. A lack of resources affects preparation by limiting the likelihood that structures will be built to withstand disasters. Response and recovery are affected as well, leaving developing nations to rely on other nations and external organizations for extensive aid.

Because resources are limited in developing nations, advances such as building roadways and utilities can take years longer than in developed nations. So when natural disasters occur in poor regions, they can wipe out decades of development in only a few hours, something which rarely happens in richer countries. According to the UN,

> *Poor people in developing countries are particularly vulnerable to disasters because of where they live. Research shows that they are more likely to occupy dangerous locations, such as flood plains, river banks, steep slopes, reclaimed land and highly populated settlements of flimsy shanty homes.*[1]

People who live in traditional structures of mud brick with heavy roofing are usually badly affected by earthquakes because these houses

"Disasters are first and foremost a major threat to development, and specifically to the development of the poorest and most [marginalized] people in the world—[disasters] ensure they stay poor."[2]
—*Didier J. Cherpitel, former secretary-general of the International Federation of Red Cross and Red Crescent Societies, 2002*

cannot withstand tremors. And poor people in developing countries may rely more on the natural environment and natural resources for survival, so when these are damaged or destroyed, these people are left without alternatives. This was the case with the 2004 Indian Ocean tsunami. The UN reported, "Disproportionately many of the victims of this disaster were poor people who depended on eco-system services and natural resources for their livelihoods."[3]

Affected on All Levels

Perhaps most striking is the difference in financial costs to nations in terms of their overall budgets, or gross domestic product (GDP). Financial losses caused by disasters tend to be greater in industrialized nations because they are more highly developed, but these costs are only a fraction of their total economy. Developing nations tend to have the opposite experience. Financial losses caused by disasters in these areas tend to be much less, but they account for a far greater percentage of developing nations' economies.

For example, Hurricane Katrina cost the United States $125 billion and the US GDP in 2005 was

*A teacher distributed school supplies to children
in a packed tent school in Haiti.*

more than $12 trillion. The cost of Katrina was
about one percent of the United States' economy
that year. In contrast, as of October 2010, the
cost of the January 2010 earthquake to Haiti was
$8 million, accounting for a larger portion of its
nearly $6.6 billion GDP (2009).

A more striking example comes from Indonesia.
Aceh is a province on the island of Sumatra, which
is part of Indonesia. Aceh was one of many places
hit by the 2004 Indian Ocean tsunami. According
to the UN, the cost of the tsunami was almost
97 percent of Aceh's GDP.

Natural disasters cause considerable economic concerns for developing nations in terms of paying for response and recovery, and in overall survival. Social development is set back considerably as funds that could or would go toward health care, education, and infrastructure must now pay for disaster relief. This is not the case—at least not to the same degree—for industrialized nations.

But disparity in wealth is not only an issue between nations. Differences in

---

Haiti versus Chile: An Earthquake Comparison

Almost seven weeks after Haiti's 7.0 earthquake in 2010, Chile experienced major seismic activity. On February 27, an 8.8 tremor hit the South American nation. The earthquake in Chile was 500 times stronger than the earthquake in Haiti, yet the death toll in Haiti was considerably higher—more than 200,000 compared to more than 795.

One reason for the difference was the location of the quake. It was offshore, farther below the surface, and in a less populated area. Another factor may be Chile's history of earthquakes. The country lies on the Ring of Fire, so tremors are common. Journalists Benjamin Witte and Sara Miller Llana addressed this issue in the *Christian Science Monitor:*

> *Because of its long history with earthquakes, which has contributed to an earthquake "consciousness" in Chile, and infrastructure that is built to higher standards, many hope that Chile will be spared the vast destruction that struck Haiti, even as it deals with one of its worst natural disasters in decades.*[4]

Haiti, however, has not had the same history with earthquakes. As such, the nation was less prepared for the tremor that occurred in January 2010. This highlights the importance of preparedness and learning from the past.

financial resources can also affect different groups of people in a single nation or city, which the devastation caused by Hurricane Katrina highlighted in New Orleans.

THE ROLE OF POVERTY IN HURRICANE KATRINA

Hurricane Katrina's victims were shown on television and in the newspapers. In New Orleans, people stood on rooftops holding signs asking for help. Many were crowded into the Superdome and in need of water and food. Residents were asked to evacuate the city, but many remained. The reason became clear in the days following Katrina's landfall.

Most of the citizens who remained in the city were living in poverty before the storm. According to the US Census Bureau, that number was 28 percent of the entire city's population. Many of the city's poor did not own a car, truck, or van. They could not simply drive away to evacuate the city. In lieu of using their own means of transportation, they could not afford to buy an airplane or bus ticket to a safer location. Without money or transportation, they had to stay and try to survive the storm.

The images seen around the world highlighted the serious problem of poverty in the United States.

Powerful Quake

According to the US Geological Survey, the force of the earthquake that caused the 2004 Indian Ocean tsunami equaled 23,000 atomic bombs.

Poverty plays a huge role in how well a person can respond to a natural disaster. A person suffering from poverty likely does not have funds set aside for an emergency—or simply savings to use in any situation. And natural disasters create unexpected costs. In order to evacuate, funds are needed to buy airplane or bus tickets or to rent a car. If a person's home is destroyed, temporary housing such as a motel will be needed, which will require money. And many things will need to be replaced, such as clothing and dishes. Most people have insurance, which will reimburse them for items lost in a natural disaster. But for people living in poverty, insurance is a luxury they cannot afford. As a result, they are left in worse conditions than those that existed before the disaster.

The stories of New Orleans and Haiti, though tragic, can have positive results in at least one respect. Studying past events is important to better understand when and where natural disasters might occur and how they might be better predicted. And analyzing what happened will help planners and responders prepare for future disasters.

WHY BUSH FAILED · CHILDREN OF THE S

Newswee

September 19, 2005 : $3.95

POVERTY, RACE & KATRINA
Lessons of A National Shame
By Jonathan Alter

The September 19, 2005, issue of Newsweek examined the role poverty and race played in the Katrina disaster and lessons to learn from it.

One way to prepare for future natural disasters is by constructing buildings better able to withstand tremors and earthquakes.

FUTURE DISASTERS

Natural disasters have existed as long as the planet, but they are changing. They have been occurring with greater frequency. While natural disasters are created by factors people cannot control, the effects of disasters may be worsening because of man-made conditions. These may magnify the effects of drought, heavy rainfall, and heat waves.

Man-Made Factors

Humans impact the environment in many ways, some of which often increase the damage resulting from natural disasters. For example, the destruction of mangrove swamps and other trees in coastal areas makes those areas more vulnerable to storm damage, since the trees would have helped minimize erosion from storm surge. And as populations increase, construction is taking place nearer these coastal zones, resulting in the further loss of trees and the destruction of protective barrier beaches by erosion.

The construction of levees and seawalls also impacts the natural processes of silting and sediment. This causes barrier beaches and islands to sink because they cannot be naturally replenished by silt deposits. In other areas, deforestation, especially in mountainous regions that usually catch water, can lead to severe flooding. Droughts are worse in places where forests and trees are gone and topsoil has eroded. But humans are affecting the environment in other ways that may influence natural disasters.

CLIMATE CHANGE

As the world moves into the twenty-first century, climate change weighs heavily on many people's minds and has become a topic of great debate at all levels. Scientists and politicians do not agree on whether the frequency of natural disasters is increasing due to climate change. Many believe global warming is a result of the release of greenhouse gases into Earth's atmosphere. For more than 200 years, humans have burned fossil fuels such as coal and oil. This has been releasing carbon dioxide and other greenhouse gases into the atmosphere. These gases act like the panels of a greenhouse and stop heat from escaping the atmosphere. While some are needed to keep the earth warm, too much could cause an unnatural change in the world's climate.

Another factor in climate change is extensive deforestation. Trees absorb excess carbon dioxide through photosynthesis. Without them, more of it remains in the atmosphere. Urban centers can also add to climate change. With a great deal of concrete and little vegetation, urban centers become heat islands. Covering the land's surfaces with bricks, buildings, and pavement makes daily temperatures

As humans cut down trees for the wood and to clear land for building, the planet is affected.

higher. Winds cannot penetrate urban landscapes to cool them as they can rolling farmlands. Dark pavement and reflective glass create more heat than trees and grass.

Some believe the argument over climate change has become exaggerated, causing unnecessary panic. And some believe climate change is part of a natural climate cycle. However, as Patrick J. Michaels and Robert C. Balling Jr. wrote in their 2009 book, *Climate of Extremes*, "Even those who claim that there is little, if any, human influence on climate do not in fact deny the existence of climate change itself."[1] Both sides of this debate do agree that temperatures are rising.

The Environmental Protection Agency predicts that Earth's temperature will rise 3.2 to 7.2 degrees Fahrenheit (5.8 to 13° C) above 1990 temperatures by the end of this century. As the temperature rises, imbalances are caused in nature. Some of these imbalances affect the environment and some affect human health. The effects include shrinking glaciers and rising sea levels, extreme temperatures, changes in where plants grow and animals live, and increased smog.

Climate change can also impact extreme weather events. Rising sea levels mean a greater risk of floods and soil erosion. Extreme temperatures can feed giant storms, increasing their size and possibly inflicting greater damage to communities. Heavier rainfall can damage crops and add to the

Climate Change and Polar Bears

Research shows that climate change is already affecting polar bears. These carnivores rely on seals as their main source of food. Polar bears hunt seals along the edge of Arctic sea ice. Climate change is melting the ice and increasing the distance between ice floes. Some bears have drowned swimming from one ice floe to another, increasing polar bear mortality. And polar bears are getting smaller. Scientists have reported that polar bears are two-thirds the size they were three decades ago. In 2008, the polar bear was added to the Endangered Species Act list of species threatened by global warming. It was the first species ever added to the list for this reason.

Natural disasters affect animals, including polar bears. Climate changes have made it more difficult for polar bears to find food.

risk of sinkholes. If global warming continues, climate zones may shift all over the world, making cooler areas more tropical and warmer areas even hotter. Heat and cold waves may increase, bringing with them opportunities for drought, flooding, or ice and snow storms. In its 2007 report, the Intergovernmental Panel on Climate Change, a scientific group that assesses climate change, concluded,

> *Human beings are exposed to climate change through changing weather patterns (for example, more intense and*

frequent extreme events) and indirectly through changes in water, air, food quality and quantity, ecosystems, agriculture, and economy. At this early stage the effects are small but are projected to progressively increase in all countries and regions.[2]

WHAT CAN WE DO?

Most natural disasters cannot be prevented, since they are a combination of weather- or geology-related factors as well as the element of chance. But steps can be taken to reduce the effects of a natural disaster. Minimizing development in coastal areas and maintaining natural features such as trees, sand dunes, and barrier beaches will reduce the destruction caused

Sea Levels

There is a normal cycle of growth and retreat of glacial ice as a glacier responds to seasonal temperature changes. But in the past decade or two, glaciers have been retreating higher up mountains and at faster rates than ever seen before. Glacial melting adds water to the seas. And with higher temperatures that force ocean water to expand, sea levels rise. It is predicted that sea levels will rise between 3.5 and 34 inches (9 and 86 cm) between 1990 and 2100.

Rising sea levels and increasing storms can cause immense damage. Coastal communities could become uninhabitable. And whole islands could become submerged. In 2005, rising sea levels forced the 100 citizens of Tégua, Vanuatu, from their island in the Pacific. It is inevitable that other islands will suffer the same fate and coastal cities could become flooded as sea levels continue to rise.

by hurricanes and flooding. Water conservation and drought-resistant lifestyles—such as minimizing agriculture and landscaping that require excessive irrigation—can help reduce the effects of drought. Using more environmentally friendly fuel sources instead of oil can reduce emissions and give people greater options if electric power outages occur.

Building structures that are more resistant to earthquakes or tornadoes can also make a difference in how severely an area is affected by a disaster. Urban planning and safer construction methods can greatly impact lives lost and property damaged in the wake of a disaster.

Nations must focus on planning and prevention in addition to response and recovery, particularly in developing countries. Anders Wijkman is a Swedish politician and a former member of the European Parliament. He addressed natural disasters in the *New York Times*:

> Industrialized countries are hit [by natural disasters] as well, but as countries become more prosperous they are better able to afford the investments needed for prevention and preparedness. A major earthquake in Iran, Turkey, or Pakistan may kill tens of thousands of people. A similar quake

in Japan or California normally kills only a few hundred at most. Better urban planning and stricter building codes explain the difference.[3]

While disaster prevention and preparedness programs may seem like luxuries in impoverished countries, studies show they ultimately save money. That is because every dollar spent on prevention saves many more dollars that would otherwise be spent on relief and reconstruction.

The Warning Signs

Since the 1990s, extreme weather events have served as evidence for those who claim that climate change is a real and pressing problem. For example, a 1,250- square-mile (3,250-sq-km) piece of the Larsen B ice shelf broke off the Antarctic Peninsula in 2002. In 2003, the Gash River in Ethiopia reached its highest level in 70 years, and 70,000 families had to leave their homes. In 2004, Brazil was hit by the first South Atlantic hurricane in history.

Natural disasters will continue around the world, but their effects can be minimized by accurate prediction, thoughtful preparation, and established systems of response and recovery. Each disaster that occurs has something to teach the world about future disasters, and it can help nations and communities prepare for those to come. Then, when disaster strikes from the skies above or the earth below, those in harm's way will be able to cope with these events as successfully as possible.

Disaster preparedness books lined the front window of a Montclair, California, bookstore in 2007 after an earthquake shook the area.

TIMELINE

79	1740s	1815
Mount Vesuvius erupts in Italy, destroying and preserving the city of Pompeii.	Archeologists begin excavating Pompeii and learn much about the daily life of Pompeians and city planning.	Mount Tambora erupts on the Indonesian island of Sumbawa and becomes the largest eruption on record.

1906	1919	1953
On April 18, San Francisco, California, is hit by a major earthquake that results in a great fire.	The International Federation of Red Cross and Red Crescent Societies is founded.	The United States officially begins naming storms.

1816	1883	1900
The Northern Hemisphere experiences a summer that is more like winter as a result of Tambora's eruption.	In August, the Indonesian island of Krakatau is completely blown apart by a volcanic eruption.	Galveston, Texas, suffers death and destruction when a hurricane strikes on September 8.

1998	2002	2004
Louisiana officials ask the US government to help develop plans for dealing with a hurricane.	An *Institute of Transportation Engineers Journal* article notes evacuation plans are inadequate for New Orleans, Louisiana.	In its review of 2003, international insurance company Munich Re addresses the role of lack of resources on the effects of disasters.

TIMELINE

2004

A tsunami in the Indian Ocean strikes 11 countries on December 26.

2005

In June, the United Nations reports on the vulnerability of developing nations to disasters.

2005

Katrina makes landfall southeast of New Orleans, Louisiana, on August 29 and devastates the city, leaving the poor as the hardest hit.

2010

On February 27, an earthquake in Chile highlights the importance of earthquake location and disaster preparation,

2010

In July, only 28,000 of the 1.5 million people left homeless by the Haiti quake have permanent housing.

2010

The effects of disasters on the poor are shown again when Pakistan experiences flooding in August.

2008

A 7.9-magnitude quake strikes Sichuan, China, highlighting the need for earthquake-resistant construction.

2009

Forty thousand families from New Orleans are still living in FEMA trailers in the aftermath of Hurricane Katrina.

2010

Haiti is devastated by an earthquake on January 12, highlighting the effects of disasters on the poor.

2010

A rare fire tornado occurs in Aracatuba, Brazil, on August 25.

2010

By August, five years after Hurricane Katrina, 98 percent of the families still living in trailers in 2009 are living in permanent housing.

2010

A cholera outbreak occurs in Haiti in October, causing more than 150 deaths and highlighting again the need for a recovery plan.

ESSENTIAL FACTS

AT ISSUE

❖ Natural disasters have caused destruction throughout history.

❖ While scientists continue to increase their understanding of geologic and meteorologic forces, they cannot predict their occurrence with 100 percent accuracy.

❖ Preparation—including mitigation—and response can limit the damage and loss of life caused by disasters.

❖ Poverty affects all facets of disaster preparation, response, and recovery. Limited resources make developing nations far more susceptible to disasters.

❖ International aid has been crucial for developing countries' recovery from disasters.

CRITICAL DATES

79

Mount Vesuvius's eruption destroyed and preserved the Roman city of Pompeii, Italy, providing a valuable resource for scientists.

1815

Mount Tambora's eruption on the island of Sumbawa, Indonesia, is the largest on record. It disrupted normal weather patterns thousands of miles away.

1906

An earthquake in San Francisco, California, caused a massive fire and great destruction. It also resulted in the first major comprehensive portrait of a US quake.

1953

The United States officially began naming storms.

1998

Louisiana officials asked the federal government to help develop plans for dealing with a major hurricane striking New Orleans.

2002

An article published in the *Institute of Transportation Engineers Journal* highlighted New Orleans's inadequate evacuation plans.

2004

In its review of 2003, international insurance company Munich Re noted the role of lack of resources on the effects of disasters.

2005

The United Nations reported on the vulnerability of developing nations to disasters. The devastation of New Orleans caused by Hurricane Katrina showed that disparities caused by wealth also occur in industrialized nations, as the majority of victims were living in poverty when the storm struck.

2010

Haiti was devastated by an earthquake in January that highlighted the effects of disasters on impoverished areas; the world immediately provided disaster relief. Chile was struck by a much stronger earthquake in February that resulted in considerably less destruction and highlighted the importance of preparation.

QUOTES

"Poor people in developing countries are particularly vulnerable to disasters because of where they live. Research shows that they are more likely to occupy dangerous locations, such as flood plains, river banks, steep slopes, reclaimed land and highly populated settlements of flimsy shanty homes."—*United Nations, "Indepth: Disaster Reduction and the Human Cost of Disaster"*

Glossary

barometer
An instrument that measures atmospheric pressure and is used in weather prediction.

breach
A gap made in a wall or fortification.

catastrophic
Having to do with a sudden or widespread disaster.

conflagration
A massive fire.

dehydrated
Deprived of moisture or water.

deploy
To arrange in a position of readiness; to make ready for use.

fault
A break or split in Earth's crust.

geologic
Having to do with geology, or the story of the earth, its rocks, and the changes it undergoes.

infrastructure
The basic systems of a country, city, or area, such as transportation, communications, power plants, and schools.

irrigation
Watering by artificial means, such as through sprinklers.

levee
An embankment designed to prevent a river or canal from flooding.

looting
Taking through dishonesty, force, or stealth; to carry off or plunder.

magnitude
Size, extent, or dimension; greatness of size or amount.

pumice
A porous or spongy form of volcanic glass.

satellite
A device designed to orbit the Earth for communications or scientific use.

seawall
A wall built to protect the shore from washing away.

seismograph
An instrument for measuring and recording the vibrations of earthquakes.

ADDITIONAL RESOURCES

SELECTED BIBLIOGRAPHY

Castleden, Rodney. *Natural Disasters That Changed the World*. Edison, NJ: Chartwell, 2007. Print.

Gibson, Christine. *Extreme Natural Disasters*. New York: Harper, 2007. Print.

Jennings, Gary. *The Killer Storms: Hurricanes, Typhoons, and Tornadoes*. New York: Lippincott, 1970. Print.

Lapham, Lewis H., ed. *The End of the World*. New York: St. Martin's, 1997. Print.

Mogil, H. Michael. *Extreme Weather: Understanding the Science of Hurricanes, Tornadoes, Floods, Heat Waves, Snow Storms, Global Warming and Other Atmospheric Disturbances*. New York: Black Dog and Leventhal, 2007. Print.

FURTHER READINGS

Barnard, Bryn. *Dangerous Planet: Natural Disasters That Changed History*. New York: Crown, 2003. Print.

Langley, Andrew. *Hurricanes, Tsunamis, and Other Natural Disasters*. New York: Kingfisher, 2006. Print.

Mark, Bonnie S. *I'll Know What to Do: A Kid's Guide to Natural Disasters*. Washington DC: Magination, 1997. Print.

Watts, Claire. *Eyewitness: Natural Disasters*. New York: Dorling Kindersley, 2006. Print.

Web Links

To learn more about natural disasters, visit ABDO Publishing Company online at **www.abdopublishing.com**. Web sites about natural disasters are featured on our Book Links page. These links are routinely monitored and updated to provide the most current information available.

For More Information

For more information on this subject, contact or visit the following organizations.

John C. Freeman Weather Museum
5104 Caroline Street, Houston, TX 77004
713-529-3076
http://www.weathermuseum.org
Visitors can explore world weather and disasters, a weather studio, world climates, and interactive weather science exhibits.

National Weather Center
120 David L. Boren Boulevard, Suite 2400, Norman, OK 73072
405-325-6933
http://www.norman.noaa.gov
This NOAA center offers a tour that includes the National Severe Storms Lab, National Weather Service Forecast Office, and the Storm Prediction Center.

Smithsonian National Museum of American History
On the National Mall, Fourteenth Street and Constitution Avenue, NW, Washington, DC
http://americanhistory.si.edu/index.cfm
The museum's collections include artifacts from Hurricane Katrina, the 1927 Mississippi River Flood, and other US disasters.

SOURCE NOTES

Chapter 1. Monster Storm

1. Wil Haygood and Ann Scott Tyson. "It Was as if All of Us Were Already Pronounced Dead." *WashingtonPost.com*. The Washington Post Company, 15 Sept. 2005. Web. 2 Nov. 2010.

2. "Anderson Cooper 360 Degrees: Special Edition: Hurricane Katrina." *CNN.com*. Cable News Network, 1 Sept. 2005. Web. 2 Nov. 2010.

3. Christine Gibson, *Extreme Natural Disasters*. New York: Harper, 2007. Print. 1.

Chapter 2. Early Disasters

1. "Mount Vesuvius." *Exploring the Environment: Volcanoes*. Wheeling Jesuit University/NASA-supported Classroom of the Future, 2004. Web. 10 Nov. 2010.

2. Andrew Wallace-Hadrill. "Pompeii: Portents of Disaster." *BBC.com*. BBC, 15 Oct. 2010. Web. 2 Nov. 2010.

3. "Archaeological Areas of Pompei, Herculaneum and Torre Annunziata." *World Heritage*. UNESCO World Heritage Centre, 2010. Web. 30 Oct. 2010.

4. Jaime McLeod. "The Year Without a Summer." *Farmers' Almanac*. Almanac, 22 Mar. 2010. Web. 29 Oct. 2010.

5. Ibid.

6. Art Chapman. "The Big One: 108 Years Ago, the Nation's Worst Natural Disaster Nearly Destroyed Galveston." *Star-Telegram*. Star-Telegram, 11 Sept. 2008. Web. 28 Oct. 2010.

7. "Jack London and the Great Earthquake and Fire." *The Virtual Museum of the City of San Francisco*. SFMuseum.org, 2007. Web. 28 Oct. 2010.

Chapter 3. Modern-Day Disasters

1. Christine Gibson, *Extreme Natural Disasters*. New York: Harper, 2007. Print. 188.

2. Paul Mann, Eric Calais, Chuck Demets, Carol S. Prentice, and Margaret Wiggins-Grandison. "Enriquillo-Plantain Garden Strike-Slip Fault Zone: A Major Seismic Hazard Affecting Dominican Republic, Haiti and Jamaica." *Jackson School of Geosciences*. University of Texas at Austin, 2008. Web. 30 Oct. 2010.

Chapter 4. Prediction

1. "Predicting Earthquakes." *USGS*. US Geological Survey, 23 Oct. 1997. Web. 30 Oct. 2010.

2. "Predicting Tornadoes: Off the Radar Screen." *Old Farmer's Almanac*. Yankee, 2010. Web. 30 Oct. 2010.

Chapter 5. Preparation

1. Todd Litman. "Lessons From Katrina and Rita: What Major Disasters Can Teach Transportation Planners." *VTPI.org*. Victoria Transport Policy Institute, 13 Apr. 2006. Web. 2 Nov. 2010.

2. "Hurricane Katrina: A Nation Still Unprepared," Executive Summary Senate Report 109-322. N.p., n.d. Web. 2 Nov. 2010.

3. "Indepth: Disaster Reduction and the Human Cost of Disaster." *Humanitarian News and Analysis*. IRIN, June 2005. Web. 31 Oct. 2010.

Source Notes Continued

Chapter 6. Response

1. Angie C. Marek. "A Post-Katrina Public Flaying." *USNews.com*. US News and World Report, 19 Feb. 2006. Web. 2 Nov. 2010.

2. Ibid.

3. "International Community Pledges Support for Haiti." *Euronews*. Euronews, 13 Jan. 2010. Web. 31 Oct. 2010.

Chapter 7. Recovery

1. "Who We Are: History." *International Federation of Red Cross and Red Crescent Societies*. N.p., n.d. Web. 31 Oct. 2010.

Chapter 8. When Resources Are Limited

1. "Indepth: Disaster Reduction and the Human Cost of Disaster." *Humanitarian News and Analysis*. IRIN, June 2005. Web. 31 Oct. 2010.

2. Ibid.

3. Ibid.

4. Benjamin Witte and Sara Miller Llana. "Chilean Earthquake: Chileans Dig Out After 8.8-Magnitude Earthquake." *CSMonitor.com*. Christian Science Monitor, 27 Feb. 2010. Web. 1 Nov. 2010.

Chapter 9. Future Disasters

1. Patrick J. Michaels and Robert C. Balling Jr. *Climate of Extremes: Global Warming Science They Don't Want You to Know*. Washington DC: Cato Institute, 2009. Print. 8.

2. "Health." *EPA.gov*. US EPA, 27 Apr. 2010. Web. 2 Nov. 2010.

3. Anders Wijkman. "We Can Minimize Natural Disasters." *New York Times*. New York Times Company, 31 Dec. 2005. Web. 2 Nov. 2010.

INDEX

About the Author

Marcia Amidon Lusted is the author of more than 40 books for young readers. She is also an editor, a writing instructor, and a musician. She lives in New Hampshire with her family.

Photo Credits

Steven Senne/AP Images, cover, 3; US Navy, Gary Nichols/AP Images, 6; Eric Gay/AP Images, 9, 97 (bottom); Christopher Mampe/Shutterstock Images, 13; iStockphoto, 14, 27; File/AP Images, 20, 97 (top); AP Images, 23, 96; The Canadian Press, Deddeda Stemler, File/AP Images, 24, 98 (top); Shutterstock Images, 31, 51, 98 (bottom); Mark Rasmussen/iStockphoto, 32; Red Line Editorial, Inc., 34; Andy Newman/AP Images, 39; Melanie Metz /Shutterstock Images, 41; Anchorage Daily News/ AP Images, 47; Claudia Dewald/iStockphoto, 48; Aaron Favila/ AP Images, 53; Lisa F. Young /Shutterstock Images, 59; Dennis Sabo/Shutterstock Images, 60; Andrea Booher/AP Images, 66; Ron Haviv/VII/AP Images, 69; Markus Schreiber/AP Images, 70; Gerald Herbert/AP Images, 75; Ariana Cubillos/AP Images, 77; Ramon Espinosa/AP Images, 78; Canadian Press via AP Images/ AP Images, 81; PRNewFoto/Newsweek/AP Images, 85; Dmitriy Shironosov/iStockphoto, 86; Mark Atkins/Shutterstock Images, 89; Erlend Kvalsvik/iStockphoto, 91; Noah Berger/AP Images, 95, 99